What can I ...?
Smell

Sue Barraclough

Heinemann
LIBRARY

Little Nippers

www.heinemann.co.uk/library
Visit our website to find out more information about **Heinemann Library** books.

To order:
☎ Phone 44 (0) 1865 888066
▤ Send a fax to 44 (0) 1865 314091
💻 Visit the Heinemann Bookshop at www.heinemann.co.uk/library to browse our catalogue and order online.

First published in Great Britain by Heinemann Library, Halley Court, Jordan Hill, Oxford OX2 8EJ, part of Harcourt Education. Heinemann is a registered trademark of Harcourt Education Ltd.

Editorial: Sarah Shannon and Louise Galpine
Design: Jo Hinton-Malivoire and Tokay,
  Bicester, UK (www.tokay.co.uk)
Picture Research: Melissa Allison
Production: Camilla Smith

Originated by Chroma Graphics (Overseas) Pte Ltd.
Printed and bound in China by South China Printing Company

ISBN 0 431 02202 X (hardback)
09 08 07 06 05
10 9 8 7 6 5 4 3 2 1

ISBN 0 431 02208 9 (paperback)
09 08 07 06 05
10 9 8 7 6 5 4 3 2 1

British Library Cataloguing in Publication Data
Barraclough, Sue
What can I? – Smell
612.8'6
A full catalogue record for this book is available from the British Library.

Acknowledgements
The Publishers would like to thank the following for permission to reproduce photographs:
Corbis p.**13** bottom; Corbis p.**17** inset (Craig Aurness), **13** top (George Shelley), **20** (Kelly-Mooney Photography); Getty Images / ThinkStock pp.**22-23**; Getty Images / PhotoDisc pp.**10**, **13** right, **21** top; Harcourt Education pp.**14-15** (Peter Evans Photography), **4-5**, **6**, **7**, **8**, **9**, **12**, **15** inset, **16-17** (Tudor Photography); Powerstock pp.**11**, **18**; Robert Harding Picture Library p.**19**; Zefa / Masterfile p.**21** right and bottom.

Cover photograph reproduced with permission of Harcourt Education Ltd. / Trevor Clifford.

Every effort has been made to contact copyright holders of any material reproduced in this book. Any omissions will be rectified in subsequent printings if notice is given to the Publishers.

Contents

Breakfast smells

Breakfast is ready. Fresh bread smells good.

What is your **favourite** breakfast smell?

Clean and fresh

Soap and toothpaste smell **fresh** and clean.

mmmmmm!

Clean socks smell **nice**.
Dirty socks smell **bad**.

Favourite smells

Banana milkshake smells **delicious.**

Sniff, sniff!

What is your favourite fruit smell?

Flowers

Butterflies and bees like flowers that smell **sweet**.

bzzzzzz!

bzzzzzz!

Do you like sweet-smelling flowers?

11

Nice smells

Perfume smells beautiful.

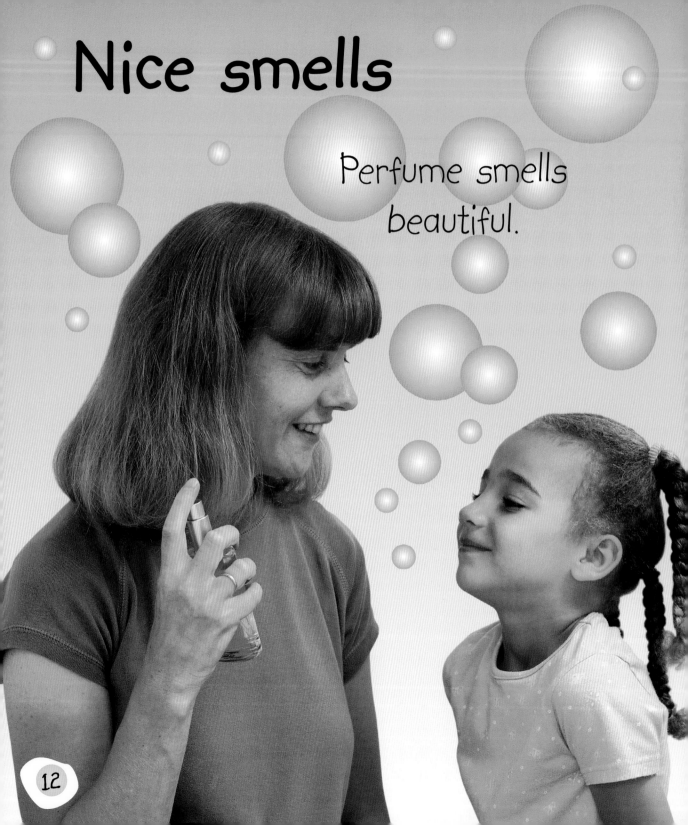

Do all these
things smell
good?

The smell is very strong. **Pooh!**

Smells delicious!

Bakers' shops sell cakes, biscuits, and bread.

Park smells

Rubbish bins smell **bad!**

What can you see
that might smell
good?

Animal noses

Look at these different animal noses.

Bedtime

A bubble bath, fresh and clean, and then a bedtime story...

Goodnight, and sweet **dreams!**

Index

Notes for adults

This series encourages children to explore their environment to gain knowledge and understanding of the things they can see, smell, hear, taste, and feel. The following Early Learning Goals are relevant to the series:

• use the senses to explore and learn about the world around them
• respond to experiences and describe, express, and communicate ideas
• make connections between new information and what they already know
• ask questions about why things happen and how things work
• discover their local environment and talk about likes and dislikes.

The following additional information may be of interest
A sniff carries air in through the nose via the nostrils into an area called the nasal cavity. The top of the nasal cavity has millions of tiny hairy cells that can detect different odours. These cells then send information to the brain for processing.

Follow-up activities
Cooking and baking activities, a walk in the park, or a shopping trip are good ways to focus on and explore different smells. Encourage children to describe a smell they can identify – perhaps by deciding if it reminds them of anything or comparing it to other smells.